CHRISTIAN MUSICIANS HANDBOOK

A BEGINNERS' GUIDE FOR SINGERS & INSTRUMENTALISTS

BY

MARY NEWLAND

ISBN 0-473-02629-5

PUBLISHED BY
MARY'S MUSIC SCHOOL

COPYRIGHT - MARY'S MUSIC SCHOOL

CONTENTS

Preface — Page 5
Forward — Page 6
Acknowledgements — Page 8

PART ONE: — Page 9

What is Singing?   Hindrances to Freedom of Expression in Singing   Anger Hurt Forgiveness   Discovering God's Plan for your Life   Four Guidance Steps   Parable of the Talents.

PART TWO: — Page 16

Posture   Upright Before the Lord   Vocal Production   Rules to Protect Vocal Chords   Vocal Exercises   Breathing.

PART THREE: — Page 26

Relaxation Technique   Healing Power of Music   Biblical History of Music   Song writing Points   Teaching with Hymns   Classical Music.

PART FOUR: — Page 35

Choreography Movement Notes   Points of Performance   Stage Introductions   The Choir & Small Group   Ministry Songs & Items   Auditions & Competitions.

PART FIVE: — Page 42

Sound Production   Microphone Techniques   Sound Systems.

PART SIX: — Page 51

Church Instrumentalists   Ministering to the Lord on the Instruments   Singing in the Spirit   Hebrew Words for Praise.

PART SEVEN: — Page 59

Requirements to Attaining Worship   What Happens when we Worship   The Song and Worship Leader.

PART EIGHT: — Page 66

Frequently Asked Questions.

PREFACE

We first came into contact with Mary's Music School after our son arranged singing lessons for himself.

Over the years we have seen the school grow in numbers and have observed the talent that has been developed in people of all ages.

Mary has a wonderful ability to encourage students in having confidence to perform in auditoriums and to develop their own individual style.

We believe that there is a need for a book of this nature and expect it to become a well used reference for those considering Christian musical ministries.

Mr & Mrs James & Margaret Newland,
Takanini, Auckland.

FORWARD

Mary Newland is of English birth and arrived in New Zealand as a child in 1964. She made a commitment to Christ in 1970 and began attending the local Presbyterian Church. A few years later she was baptised in water and the Spirit, and became a member of the Queen Street Assembly of God. Since Mary and Philip married, they attended Mt. Albert Baptist Church and in 1993 moved to West City Christian Centre.

In 1977 Mary attended Faith Bible College in Tauranga which began her training for the ministry of music. After this, Mary returned to Auckland and worked as a bank officer for several years, during which time she pursued both vocal and theory studies. Her teachers entered Mary in both The Royal School of Music and Trinity College of Music exams in practical vocal and theory of music sections. Mary can now sing both classical and contemporary styles of music.

In 1982 Mary was accepted to tour with the Continental Singers which is an American christian singing group based in California. She completed two tours with the first visiting the U.S.A, Spain, Greece and France; And the second to Fiji, Australia and New Zealand. This was a major breakthrough for Mary in the singing realm and also taught her much about leadership skills. The tours lasted for six months and then she returned to N.Z. knowing that she would go back to the U.S.A. to do some biblical studies as soon as possible.

In 1984, eighteen months later, Mary returned to the U.S.A. to study at Christ for the Nation Institute in Dallas Texas (CFNI). This is the school founded by the well known author Gordon Lindsay. The year of study there taught Mary many things including the spiritual side of singing. It was during the last semester there that the call to start a teaching and singing ministry came. Mary was at a local south Dallas church where a very anointed lady minister was having a crusade that was in its third week. During one evening service she called Mary into the isle and began to give a word of prophesy, and the anointing of the Lord came upon her to do this work. The leaders of C.F.N.I. school confirmed this word and also prayed with her. One of Mary's fellow students said that she would go home and begin "Mary's Music School" and she stored it away in her heart. In June 1985 Mary graduated and returned home.

In July 1985 Mary's Music School began, part time until the end of that year, and then full time from the beginning of 1986. The school has grown and developed well over the years.

Mary has been singing as soloist since she returned from C.F.N.I. in 1985 and has performed in both small and large church gatherings including the Town Hall and Beaumont Street auditorium. Mary has a good selection of backing tapes that she usually uses and can provide a good sound system for small halls. Her husband Philip does the sound work for her concerts. Mary's concert aims are that music is used as a ministry tool to open doors for people to receive Gods word, provide healing and bring people into a relationship with Jesus.

Mary was married to Philip Newland in october 1989. Her husband Philip is a radio technician by trade and an accomplished sound technician. Philip has also travelled with Youth With A Mission (Y.W.A.M.) for two years on their ships working in the area of electronics. Mt. Albert Baptist Church was his home church.

The aims of Mary's Music School is; to teach christians in the Auckland area how to sing correctly and enhance the praise and worship in their churches. Also to develop the best results possible with the deposits of talent each individual has received. To encourage each student to develop their spiritual relationship with the Lord and find their ministry abilities.

The two main avenues through which these aims are achieved, are private lessons and concerts. The teaching is both practical and spiritual, and develops the full three areas of the individual; body, soul and spirit that are involved in the christian singing ministry. Mary has found that counselling in these areas is often required and she endeavours to assist the students where needed. Students are provided with as many practical outlets to sing as possible. During the third term the end of year christmas concerts are worked on by the students, which teaches them performance techniques.

ACKNOWLEDGEMENTS

Special Thanks are offered to the following people who gave many good lectures and teachings during my years of training.

The staff of the Continental Singers in California in 1982

The staff at Christ For the Nations Bible School. (Dallas 1985)

Philip Newland, my husband, for his experience and expertise in the Sound Techniques, Typesetting and also his encouragement and support as I prepared this material.

EDITIONS; Paper - 2/87, 4/88, 5/89, 7/96, 9/05,
E-Book 3/2015

UNAUTHORIZED REPRODUCTION of this book or any part thereof is PROHIBITED.
© 1987 Mary Newland.

PART ONE

WHAT IS SINGING?

Singing is a personal expression of oneself from the inside to the outside. The feelings and emotions are involved.
Singing is initiated by the Spirit, comes through the Soul, and is expressed by the Body. All three parts of man are involved; and all three areas need to be taken care of properly and disciplined.

HEBREWS 4 v 12 "For the Word of God is living and active, sharper than any two-edged sword, piercing to the division of soul and spirit, of joints and marrow, and discerning the thoughts and intentions of the heart".

THE SPIRIT; Of man needs to be filled with the Holy Spirit of God and control given over to Him. The Spirit needs to be fed daily by the *Word & Prayer* and kept free from sin.

THE SOUL; Of man needs to be free from the bondages of sin, guilt, unforgiveness, hurts and other crippling bruises of Satan in our lives. This area must be kept free if a person is to have freedom to worship the Lord in Song. Good relationships are a necessity here. One needs to seek to have an upright attitude in heart towards others.

HEBREWS 12 v 14 "Strive for peace with all men, and for the holiness without which no one will see the Lord."

THE BODY: Of man must be kept pure and well looked after. Keep it fit and healthy, eat & sleep well. Be upright in stature and in morals, remember not to pollute God's temple that He has chosen for us to dwell in. Portray Gods goodness in dress and behaviour - remember you are a "child of the King"!

HINDRANCES TO FREEDOM OF EXPRESSION IN SINGING

1. When Satan attacks the Soul area with various forms of crippling devices such as; rejection, bitterness, hatred, insecurity, and fear.

2. When Satan attacks the Spirit area through pride, selfishness, and rebellion.

3. If Satan can get a place in the emotional area of a person He can control that person; Eg. fear. The emotional being of man is formed without his conscious knowledge or choice. He can be victimized, hurt, and bound emotionally by others whom the enemy uses as instruments.

4. Both man and Satan are spiritual beings, and the enemy has access to man through this avenue. The emotional bruises which Satan inflicts are often strong contributing factors to mans spiritual problems and sometimes can affect the emotions and physical well being.

5. Your part as a singer is to be a clean and prepared vessel. Voice training involves much discipline and practice. We are called to be minstrels unto the Lord. See 1 Chronicles 15 starting at verse 16 where David told the leaders of the Levites to appoint musicians and singers.

ANGER HURT & FORGIVENESS

" We may not be responsible for the event that caused our pain, but we are responsible always for our response to the event that caused our pain". Many people would rather maintain their rage than apply forgiveness.

Anger is holding someone under an obligation to suffer for what they have done to you. It is always revenge and punishment orientated.

4 WAYS YOU CAN DEAL WITH ANGER

1. You can **EXPRESS** it: Aggressively

2. You can **REPRESS** it: Denying myself and others

3. You can **SUPPRESS** it: Acknowledge it but don't express it

4. You can **CONFESS** it: Express the pain and not blame the other person. Confession of the pain and learning to accept the pain as your own is the best way to deal with it. You are responsible for your own actions and reactions.

PAST HURTS IN 4 CATEGORIES

REJECTION   SEXUAL ABUSE   BEING PUT DOWN   LOSS

If you respond sensitively, or react angrily without much cause, or withdrawing from a situation, then these are all signs that you need to overcome an area of hurt in your life. To choose to act independently of God is to remain angry. We need to choose to act with God's ways to forgive.

FORGIVENESS

Forgiveness is to stop seeking Revenge and stop Blaming them for the anger. Learn from the experience.

FIVE STEPS TO FORGIVENESS

1. Take ownership of your negative emotions, and be responsible for your own actions. God teaches self control and a sense of responsibility.

2. Identify the sins or wrong behaviour that you may be directing against others as a result of negative emotions.

3. Accept forgiveness for the sins or wrong behaviour that you may have done to others.

4. Forgive the person you are angry at or the one we blame for the way we are at present.

5. Raise up the negative memory as a memorial to the healing instead of a memorial to the pain.

REPENTANCE

This is a very important word in the line of forgiveness. Do something in line with God's will; Forgive. For example "The Prodigal Son" (Luke 15; 11 to 32).

FORGIVENESS BEGINS THE PROCESS OF INNER HEALING

RESULTS OF FORGIVENESS

1. You can feel very vulnerable as you have no way to protect yourself from any more hurt.

2. You can sense a feeling of injustice. We forgive because Christ forgave us and tells us to do the same.

3. It can trigger the release of deep pain. Allow yourself to feel the pain and let it surface. It won't destroy you even though it may feel like it. Through this process there is a danger that you may revert back to blame again, if so go through the process again.

4. Learn not to wear another persons guilt.

This diagram shows a pictorial description of the process of Anger and its related disorders

DISCOVERING GOD'S PLAN FOR YOUR LIFE

1. AM I CALLED BY GOD TO SING?

Revelation 17 v 14 "They will make war on the Lamb, and the Lamb will conquer them, for He is Lord of Lords and King of Kings, and those with Him are *called chosen and faithful*".

2. GOD'S CALL FOR YOU IS:

A) ETERNAL

Jeremiah 1 v 5 "Before I formed you in the womb I knew you, and before you were born I consecrated you..."

eternity past   NOW   eternity future

You are **no** accident in God!

B) REVEALED PROGRESSIVELY

God's plans are revealed step by step, as we obey, and is usually in general terms so that we can accept it and understand. Our lack of faith and being human limits us to what we can accept and believe. As you progress, more details are revealed. There is a definite time of preparation and training which can be many years.

Isaiah 49 v 1 & 2 "The Lord knew me from the womb, from the body of my mother He named my name. He made my mouth like a sharp sword, in the shadow of His hand He hid me, he made me a polished arrow in His quiver, He hid me away."

The arrows must be prepared, polished, straight and very smooth so that when they are sent out they hit the mark targeted. This is a very important time of preparation.

Jonah 3 v 1
"The word of the Lord came to Jonah a second time saying..."

When the call of God comes a second time, it is different and deeper, often born out of pain and suffering. God is merciful to us if we mess up. Confession and seeking His will again will get you back on course. You need to spend the waiting time preparing and developing your talents. The parable of the wise and foolish virgins with their lamps show this principle. See Matthew 25 v 1 to 13.
So don't wait until you're given opportunities to sing before you start with lessons!

FOUR GUIDANCE STEPS

1. The Witness of God in your heart. Be led by the Holy Spirit. Learn to exercise your senses by experiences and use. Practice sensing the presence, and hearing the word of God daily.

2. The Wisdom of God. Get Wisdom. Listen to those who walk with God. Proverbs 4 v 7 "The beginning of wisdom is this; Get Wisdom and whatever you get, get insight."

3. The Word of God. Read and study God's Word faithfully. Psalm 119 v 105 "Thy word is a lamp to my feet and light to my path."

4. The Works of God. God makes the way for you. He opens and closes doors. A closed door can be a real blessing and is often shut by the mercy of God, so don't try to knock it down!

KEYS TO DISCOVERING GOD'S WILL FOR YOU.

Romans 12 v 1 & 2 "Do not be conformed to this world but be transformed by the renewing of your mind, that you may prove what is the Will of God; what is GOOD, ACCEPTABLE and PERFECT."

Anywhere, any time and any place God's Will is Good to you, it is acceptable or pleasing to you, and perfect it will fit into everything and suit your circumstances.

AM I CHOSEN BY GOD TO SING?

Isaiah 48 v 10 "Behold I have refined you, but not like silver, I have tried you in the furnace of affliction."

To be chosen you need to go through the preparation time which is often the furnace of affliction. It is in this time that Satan's aim is to destroy you. Under the heat of adversity the impurities and less valuable qualities come out. When God is dealing with us He takes away not just the dross, but also things that would detract from His purposes. They may seem to be good to us, but a distraction to God's will.

AM I FOUND FAITHFUL TO SING?

If through all this time you have endured, you shall stand victorious. One day the Lord will send you out like a straight arrow to hit the mark for His purposes. It takes God's time and our patience! Nothing happens in our time unless it is God ordained.

PARABLE OF THE TALENTS: MATTHEW 25 V 14 to 30.

I have seen many students come and go. Some have a large deposit of talent and ability while others only a small amount. I rarely turn anyone away because I feel it is what each one does with what they have been given, not the amount that counts. Very often the gifted students waste their abilities by not practising. They think that they will get by, and sadly they often do. They end up staying on one level and not developing to their full potential available to them in the Lord.

Sometimes people come for lessons just so that they can say "But I'm having singing lessons" to others in church as a status symbol.
My answer is; "soap is no good unless it is applied!"
Time usually reveals true attitudes.

I also see the ones that have a very small deposit of ability who struggle to just get the notes in a song correct. They work and work, and in the end they do finish receiving their reward. Maybe those that have only a little ability think that what they have is not enough to work with especially when they compare themselves with others more gifted around them. God's Word says definitely that it is not wise to compare yourself with others.

2 Corinthians 10 v 12 "We do not dare to classify or compare ourselves with some who commend themselves. When they measure themselves by themselves and compare themselves with themselves, they are not wise."

The Lord rewarded those who used and developed their abilities and talents sending away the ones that hid their only gift. It is of great frustration to a singing teacher to see gifted people wasting their talents instead of perfecting and developing them and becoming more useful to the Lord and his purposes.

PART TWO

TECHNICAL ASPECTS OF SINGING

POSTURE

The following scripture references deal with "Being Upright" in these areas. They would make a good home-group bible study.

    Physical   Moral   Spiritual   Verbal

Leviticus 26;13
1 Chronicles 29;17
Psalm 11;7
Psalm 20;7,8
Psalm 25;8,21
Psalm 33;1,4
Psalm 36;10
Psalm 64;10
Psalm 92;12-15
Psalm 97;11
Psalm 111;7-8
Psalm 112;1-4
Psalm 119;7,137
Psalm 125;4
Psalm 140;13
Proverbs 2;21
Proverbs 10;9,29
Proverbs 11;3,6,11
Proverbs 12;6
Proverbs 14;2,9,11
Proverbs 15;8,19
Proverbs 16;17
Proverbs 21;18,19
Proverbs 28;10,18
Proverbs 29;27
Ecclesiastes 7;29
Isaiah 33;15

POSTURE

1. PHYSICAL Your standing between God & Man.

Ecclesiastes. 7 v 29 "This only have I found: God made mankind upright, but men have gone in search of many schemes."

God made man to walk upright in the beginning. The physical structure of man has an upright spinal column. Correct sitting, standing and bending are important for both general health and for all those involved in any public ministry. All aspects of singing are dependent on correct posture and include, breathing, diction, etc.

2. MORAL Your standing in your relationship with others before God.

1 Chronicles. 29 v 17 (RSV) "I know my God, that thou triest the Heart, and hast pleasure in uprightness, in the uprightness of my heart I have freely offered all these things."

Proverbs. 10 v 9 (RSV) "He who walks in uprightness walks securely, but he who perverts His ways will be found out."

Christians should stand up for the principles written in the Word of God for our guidance and instruction. God's Word is not "old- fashioned" or "out of date" but it is "the same yesterday today and forever." We need more conviction and holiness in the church today. Too many people are profaning God's temple and are still expecting God to bless and reward them regardless of their sins.

A correct and true reverential fear of the Lord needs to be taught in the church today, especially amongst the young people. To minister in song the vessel needs to be clean, holy and sanctified for Gods' use; or the sacrifice will be stained and unclean, therefore unacceptable.

3. SPIRITUAL Your standing in your relationship towards God.

Proverbs 10 v 29 (RSV) "The Lord is a stronghold to him whose way is upright, but destruction to the evil-doer."

Psalm. 119 v 7 (RSV) "I will praise thee with an upright heart, when I learn of thy righteous ordnances."

Psalm. 64 v 10 (AMP) "The uncompromisingly righteous shall be glad in the Lord and shall trust and take refuge in Him, and all the upright in heart shall glory and offer praise."

How is your communication with the Lord? Are there any hindrances in the way? Is the Lord, Lord of all or are there other people, other things, blocking the way? You cannot expect your singing to carry the anointing and ministry of God if your devotions are not directed to him alone. God will not share His Glory with others.

4. VERBAL Your standing in your speech before God.

2 Corinthians. 10 v 12 (NIV) "We do not dare to classify or compare ourselves with some who commend themselves. When they measure themselves by themselves and compare themselves with themselves they are not wise."

Can you guard your tongue? Do you tell the whole truth always? Control of the tongue needs to be surrendered to the Holy Spirit, to be used for His work in praise and song. In singing the tongue must be trained to produce correct sounds and to be an asset to the singers voice in diction and breathing. A study of the life of Job will show a man who was called "blameless and upright" Job 1;1,8. 2;3,10.
All three aspects of man; Body, Soul and Spirit are involved in singing and need to be cleansed from sin - upright before the Lord.

"Minstrels unto the Lord" are people that must be sanctified in these areas. It is a very responsible position, not to be taken lightly, or abused, lest God's judgement falls upon the church concerned.

VOCAL PRODUCTION

VOICE SOUND
Is produced by the larynx and speech is the sound formed into words by the tongue and lips. The accessory air sinuses act as resonators. A whisper is speech without voice, and in whispering there is no vibration of the vocal chords.

THROAT TONES
A common problem is that the singer tends to sing from the throat area, and tries to get volume by putting pressure in this area. This creates loss of high notes and strength also putting unwanted stress on the vocal chords. If the sound is throttled, airy and restricted it is probably coming from the throat area.

HEAD TONES
If the tone is clear, light, and freely resonating, it is coming from the front of the face near the cheek bones or higher more in the forehead A very forward tone will vibrate on the lips and face as the air rushes past them making the lips quiver; the " oo " vowel is a good example of this. A high note sung forward and placed in the top of the head will resonate and can be heard inside your head as the tones travel around the sinuses through the air passages. Sopranos can often experience this with their high notes.

DIAPHRAGM
Volume comes from here and not the throat area. A controlled push of air from the diaphragm will send the note stronger out to resonate in the sinus area and create more volume. " EE " is a good vowel to practice this on a lower high note. The chest area is the

resonator for the low notes and gives depth and solidity of sound especially for men's baritone and bass areas.

THE LARYNX
This is the organ of the voice. With the vocal chords brought together in a straight line they can be caused to vibrate in a blast of expired air, this is how sound is produced. Variation in pitch is produced by varying the tension of the vocal chords. They can be tightened or relaxed by the muscles attached to the cartilages of the larynx. The greater the tension of the vocal chords the higher the note that results.

THE TONGUE
Needs to be trained in singing to lie flat down to the bottom of the mouth with the tip behind the bottom teeth, and the back of the tongue as flat as possible. This position allows the voice to come through as clearly and unrestricted as possible. This could take 2 to 3 weeks to master but is well worth the effort involved.

THE SOFT PALATE AND UVULA
The top back of the mouth and the piece of skin hanging down in the centre back are these two areas. They need to be tightened and lifted up, out of the way of the air flow that comes up the throat. The lifting sensation can be felt in a yawn, and these muscles are then used to lift when we need to sing high notes. The large space created when the area is lifted gives fullness and volume to the voice and helps to cut out any airiness once the sound is directed into the head.

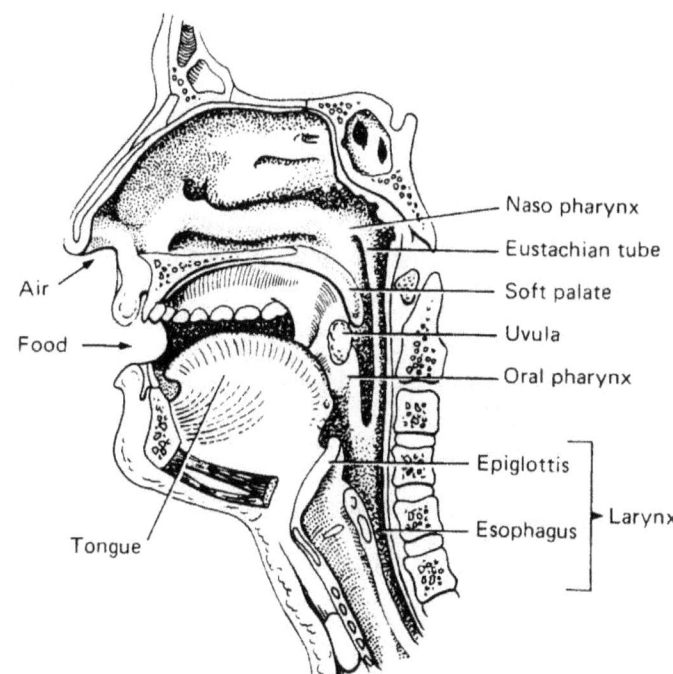

Sagittal section of mouth and nose

RULES TO PROTECT VOCAL CHORDS

1. When talking to others always be within one meter of them unless you can use an amplifying system. Try to avoid shouting, yelling, screaming, cheering, and excessive loud laughing. Instead wave or clap your hands or use gestures and noise makers like a whistle to express yourself.

2. So you can be heard easily, sit in the centre of a room or group, and speak only when others are quiet. Talk at the best pitch with a good rate and adequate loudness. Place your voice correctly; that is not too high or low, and avoid strong nasal or throat tones.

3. Do not make strange noises with your voice, and cough, sneeze, or clear your throat only when you must.

4. Try not to talk in noisy places: like around machines, lawn mowers, hair dryers, stereos, motorbikes and fast wind activities.

5. Hold your head straight when you talk and make sounds effortlessly and smoothly. Keep your face, throat, neck and shoulders relaxed as you speak and have enough breath as you talk.

6. Some spicy foods, whole milk, ice cream, nuts and dry flaky foods can cause voice problems.

7. When you have a cold, or laryngitis, avoid much talking and breathing through your mouth especially in cold weather. Try to have filtered heating, air conditioning and proper humidity in your house and work area.

8. Follow a balanced nutritious diet and exercise regularly. Do not smoke and stay away from smoky or dusty places. Get enough sleep.

9. Check to be sure that any regular medications have no undesirable effects, especially dryness in the throat, mouth and nose. Sometimes a complete vocal rest is needed or a reduced amount of talking or singing. This is to give the voice time to recover from strains and viruses from colds and flu.

VOCAL EXERCISES

Try singing these words to a scale of medium range (middle C to C), if you don't have an exercise CD.

1) hum chew..... to loosen the jaw muscles and get flexibility.

2) ee or ee or ee or.....

3) ah lay loo yah.....

4) me ah me ah me.....

5) e ver lar sting.....

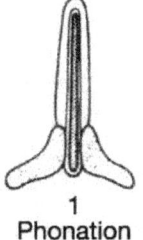
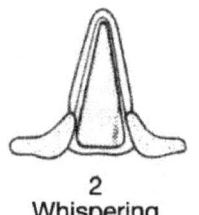
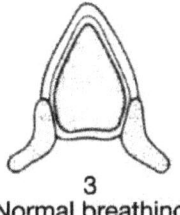

1 Phonation   2 Whispering   3 Normal breathing

6) Hold your tongue out of mouth with your fingers then slide slowly and gently up and down the scale from the very bottom of your range to the top and back down again. This is especially good for men to smooth out the breaks in their voice.

7) Short " ME ME " Exercise; Do a very high pitch short strong "me me "sound and think the air up behind the bridge of the nose. It should "explode" and vibrate there with no trouble! These are very resonant sinuses.

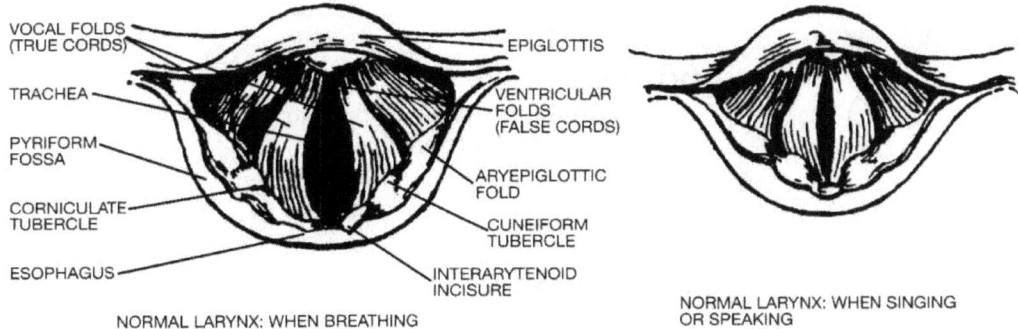

NORMAL LARYNX: WHEN BREATHING   NORMAL LARYNX: WHEN SINGING OR SPEAKING

VOWEL SHAPES AND FINGER SPACES BETWEEN TEETH

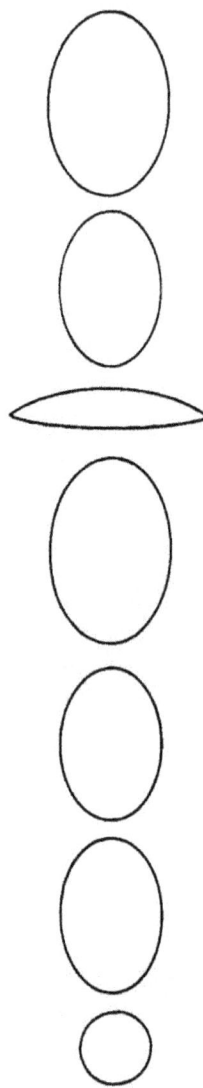

AH 3 finger spaces
large vertical oval shape

AY 2 finger spaces
medium vertical oval shape

EE 1 finger space
small horizontal oval shape.

OH 3 finger spaces
large vertical oval shape with lips
forward to project sound outward.

OR 2 finger spaces
medium vertical oval shape with lips
forward.

ER 2 finger spaces
medium vertical oval shape with lips
forward.

OO 1 finger space
small round whistle shape with inside of mouth lifted up
to get sound forward and out.

BREATHING

Breathing in is carried out by means of muscular movements which increase the lung capacity of the chest. The increasing capacity of the chest draws air into the lungs through air passages. The action may be compared with drawing air into a pair of bellows and forcing it out again. The diaphragm contracts and tightens increasing the capacity of the chest. The intercostal muscles contract and raise the ribs to a horizontal position increasing the diameter of the chest as it moves outwards.

BREATHING EXERCISES

1. Stand upright and raise your hands to the Lord into the praise position. This immediately raises the rib-cage and gives room for the lungs to expand freely. Let your shoulders stay down and level, not up or forward. Slowly bring your hands down to rest on the front lower area of your ribs. Leave your ribs in the upright position and keep your shoulders level. (Now you are ready to sing!)

2. Now breathe slowly in - using your tummy areas (diaphragm and intercostal muscles). As the air goes in, the area of the waistline and abdomen flatten and tighten. These muscles need to be strong and able to maintain pressure to control air flow and volume. It is very important to keep the tummy area strong and not flabby! I recommend a course of abdominal exercises from your local Gym to help you here. (Flabby tummy muscles means a flabby voice!)

3. **It is best to lie down on the floor to do the following exercises.** This takes care of posture and keeps you from falling if you get dizzy or light headed through the extra intake of oxygen!
a) Breathe in twice with a slow sipping sound and out twice with a hiss; (this helps you hear the air going in and out).

b) Make four in and out counts. Be careful to get rid of all the air as you breathe out.

c) Do short separated two in and two out breaths at a moderate pace.

d) Try four short separated in and out breaths at a faster pace.

e) Then try an eight count in and out at a quicker pace. Always remember to control the timing and keep the ribs up. Do not use the chest or shoulders for breathing.

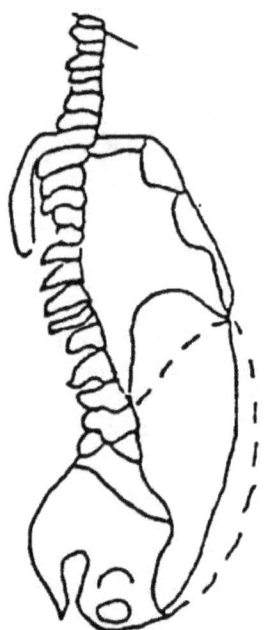

Body diagram
of breathing

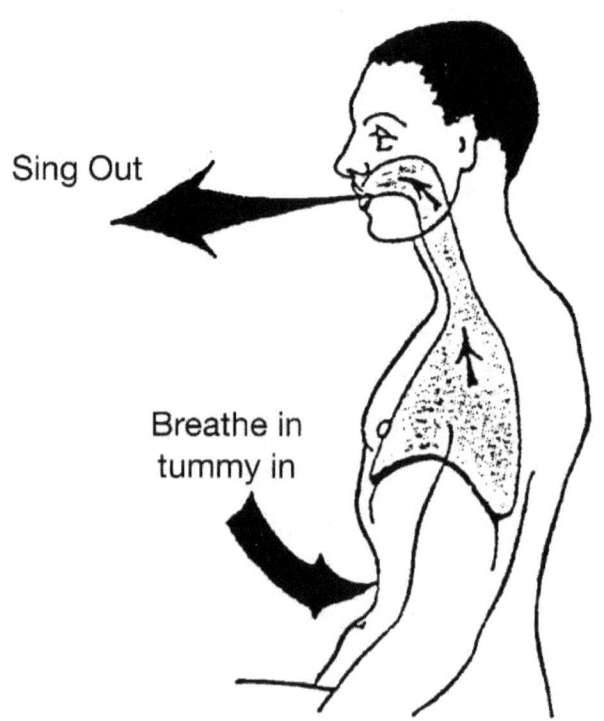

Sing Out

Breathe in
tummy in

PART THREE

RELAXATION TECHNIQUE

Muscle relaxation can be used effectively to lower tension in the body and eliminate the symptoms of stress.

Relaxation of the muscles leads to relaxation of the mind, not to produce sleep but if practised when alert the process will result in a feeling of a calm alertness rather than drowsiness.

It is therefore good to do before any performance to get nerves under control! Deep breathing exercises also are good to do before a performance.

> 1) Lay down on a firm surface such as a carpet floor. Remove glasses and tight clothing should be loosened. Lay on your back with the spine straight, feet comfortably apart, hands just out from your sides and palms up, and close eyes.
>
> 2) First tense all your muscles and then go limp. Play some soft string based music as you do this (Praise Strings). Lay still and don't move any part of the body as it sinks into the floor.
>
> 3) Breathe slowly and deeply as you do this and keep listening to the music not letting the mind wander onto things to be done that day.
>
> 4) Slowly open eyes and bend one leg up then the other. Then slowly lift yourself up with your arms and sit up.

This is a very good way to relax during the day, or before going to sleep after a very busy stressed out day!

THE HEALING POWER OF MUSIC

Music has the power and ability to set our minds and spirit free from fatigue and nervous tension. It has the capacity to be used in a positive way to restore physical health and mental disorders.

MUSIC THERAPY

Music is used in hospitals to treat arthritis, spastic-paralysis, and heart fatigue as well as mental disorders. Music brings back forgotten memory associations very quickly, as a song can trigger an idea, thought, colour, or sound, or a picture of things lost in the past. Think of a busy harassed day, and you come home all tensed up emotionally. If you play a soothing quiet recording you will soon find the pressure lifts and things seem not so bad after all! But if you had played a fast up tempo record it probably wouldn't help you at all, and could even make you worse!

SAUL is a very good example.
Saul was bothered by an evil spirit and had no peace of mind. When David played his harp the anointed music brought peace and rest to his troubled mind and body. 1 Samuel 16 v 14 to 23. It was the presentation of an anointed song by a skilful musician that delivered Saul from an evil spirit. The Anointing is what made the difference here to set Saul free from the demonic influences upon him.

ANOINTED MUSIC

We as Christians are often under spiritual attack by Satan and many times don't realize it until too late. If we learn to detect this influence and play anointed music in our homes we will find great release of pressure, tension and oppression in our lives.

As Singers we should aim to keep ourselves free from these influences as much as we can, and also to strive to have the anointing upon our own music performance. One needs to be careful what sort of music to listen to, and when to listen to it. A rocky piece will not help one go to sleep, whereas a quiet gentle piece would calm the emotions down ready for sleep.

In Church Services the anointing should be so present in the music that people get healed both physically and emotionally from just being in its presence.

Music can also bring sickness upon a person, loud music can cause ulcers, insomnia, and heart trouble; and bring intense pain upon the body. Music can make you hyper, hypnotize and put you to sleep. It has been proven that certain sound waves low enough in frequency can even kill you. Music can be a tremendous destructive or tremendous healing force. Let us be responsible with our music to bring healing to the people whom we minister to, and bring peace and deliverance through the music played in the name of our Lord.

BIBLICAL HISTORY OF MUSIC - MUSIC IN THE BEGINNING

Before the creation of the earth and man, God had a Heaven and Angels. The three archangels that had most authority and responsibility were; Michael, Gabriel, and Lucifer. Michael is a warrior and protector and Gabriel is a messenger. Lucifer was the chief musician who had tambourines and pipes built into his body. Ezekiel 28 v 12 to 20 tells about Lucifer and his fall from Heaven. Lucifer was very skilled at playing the instruments that were built into him, and he had a very important role in Heaven. He was to lead the Angelic hosts in singing and playing. Isaiah 14 v 11 says "Your pomp is brought down to sheol, the sound of your harps." When he fell his music fell also and became music of the grave, Hell. Music in the beginning was ordained by God and was pleasing to Him. It was given or created to minister to God the Father. MUSIC WAS CREATED TO WORSHIP GOD and not for any other secular purpose or even for evangelism, although it can be used to reach the unsaved.

Lucifer was a worship leader and was very wise and beautiful. Ezekiel. 28 v 13. Lucifer began to desire worship for himself, and this rebellion caused God to throw Lucifer down to earth and a third of the angels went with him. Revelation 12 v 3,7 & 9; 2 Peter 2 v 4; Luke 10 v 18 "I beheld Satan as a lightning fall from Heaven." THE DAY LUCIFER FELL, MUSIC FELL AND THERE BECAME MUSIC THAT HAD AN EARTHLY NATURE and became music of the world instead of appealing to God and the spiritual man. Lucifer's desire for worship is still around and he still uses his musical gifts and abilities to get worship because he craves it. Isaiah 14 v 13 & 14..

Music is considered by God as important and it is mentioned in the Bible over 839 times. God chose Singing for His people to come into His presence. Psalm 100 v 2. "Serve the Lord with gladness, come into His presence with Singing." The Singers were part of the ministry staff of the church in the Old Testament. The Song Service is not just a preliminary, an icebreaker, or to warm the people with. Singing is a prerequisite for the word of God to be received. Music breaks down barriers and softens hearts. There are over 200 scriptures that tell us to sing. Psalms 96 v 1; 147 v 7; Ephesians 2 v 2; 3 v 10; 5 v 18 & 19.

TWENTY SONGWRITING POINTS

1. FORM; Songs need a structural pattern both in the music and in the lyrics. General styles are: verse chorus verse (A - B- A), or A -A - B - B, EG; "He Touched Me" is A - B - A.

2. SUBJECT: Make a point and stick to it. eg "Because He lives."

3. PROGRESSION; Be logical, beginning, middle, climax, end. Both in the music and the message, eg "To God be the Glory."

4. REPETITION: There needs to be repetition of lyrics, melody, rhythm, and the use of melodic sequences. A level of at least Grade 3 music Theory study would help here.

5. HOOK: The element that grabs attention. In lyrics, melody, rhythm, instrumental, production, and performance.

6. EMOTIONAL IMPACT: Sets the mood of the song and the atmosphere. It needs to be consistent in verses and contrasted in choruses. Dramatic songs need to be in a suitable key for the singer, to give energy to the song. Match the intensity of the singer to the intensity of the song.

7. DIRECTNESS: Establish quickly the problem, person, or place, eg; "Jesus there's just something about that Name."

8. UNITY Vs VARIETY: Repetition is an element of unity, and variety is given in change of melody.

9. DISTILLED LYRICS: Write and rewrite lyrics, make them short and descriptive pictures with no unnecessary words, use action words, use conversational lyrics, except for effects.

10. LYRICS EASY TO HEAR: Make differences obvious; eg; a theatrical song and a congregational song.

11. LYRICS EASY TO SING: Use flowing vowel sounds, avoid "s". Lyrics are to be intelligible, clear and without requiring explanation.

12. AVOID CLICHES: Be fresh and grammatically correct. Do not use local words or slang.

13. THEOLOGY: Should be scripturally and theologically correct. If in doubt check it out with your Pastor.

14. IDENTIFIABLE: Deal with things and subjects that others can relate to easily.

15. CONTEMPORARY SETTING: Be in a current style of music.

16. MUSIC: Make the music enhance and build the words, not drowning them out with too many instruments or difficult timing.

17. SIMPLE: Keep it simple avoid too many complex elements.

18. RANGE: Don't make the range more than eleven notes between lowest and highest note of the melody so that the congregation can join in if required.

19. TITLES: Make them short and descriptive so they can be easily remebered. The first line of the chorus is often used.

20. SPIRITUAL CONTENT: Must be correct, and able to be anointed.

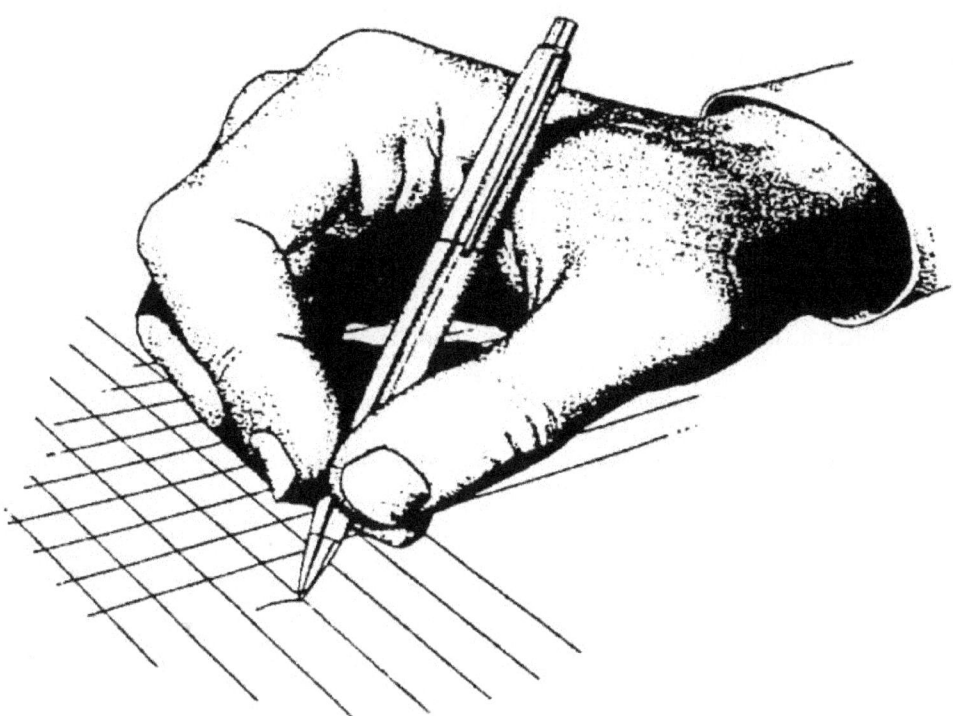

TEACHING WITH HYMNS

MATTHEW 13 V 52
"Therefore every scribe which is instructed unto the Kingdom of Heaven is like unto a man that is an householder, which bringeth forth out of his treasure things new and old."

The Charismatic Movement has brought into our worship the new scripture choruses and singing in the spirit, but can frequently bring an inclination to "throw out the hymn books in favour of new songs." There has also been a shift in the emphasis on praise choruses to a genuine exaltation of the character of God; His power, majesty, and glory.

Hymns and older songs can be used to teach spiritual truths to the congregation who sing them with open hearts and minds. Musical sermons are found in songs such as; "What a Friend we have in Jesus", "O for a Thousand Tongues", and "All hail the power of Jesus' Name."

Hymns, which are often passed over in favour of a more contemporary song, are rich in quality of text and message. Many Hymns were written in times of stress and trial for the author.

The Hymn "A Mighty Fortress is our God" was written during a peak in Martin Luther's struggle against the Roman Church. The song takes it's title from Psalm 46 "God is our refuge and strength" and the truths expressed in this great hymn have not lost their meaning and relevancy even with the passage of time.
The song "It is well with my soul", was born out of great personal tragedy, and by noting key phrases of a hymn to your congregation, you can emphasize ideas that will uplift and strengthen them as they sing.

Try to co-ordinate both new choruses and old hymns to put together a theme that will correspond or compliment a particular teaching or occasion. Also use transparencies to teach songs and hymns not found in the hymnal and to eliminate the distraction of finding "song number X". You can ask the congregation to read through the words while the pianist plays quietly, which encourages them to be more responsive in praise and worship.

CLASSICAL MUSIC AND CONTEMPORARY MUSIC.

I have often had students ask me about Classical music and find generally that there is a generation growing up now that know very little about the "Old Masters". The question of whether a Christian should listen to, and or sing classical styles is sometimes asked and I find that there are no set laws in scripture about it. If listening to some Bach or Beethoven gives you inspiration and pleasure that is not contrary to God's Word, then I say it's O.K. To learn to sing or play such music takes much skill and mastery of the instrument so it would be to your credit and an asset to your ministry talent to learn. There is an art to singing a classical piece because it is much harder by the very composition and arrangement of the music. In the process of learning such a piece it would develop your technical abilities and be advantageous to your ministry in song.

Contemporary music is written simpler and therefore easier to sing or play deliberately; so that the general congregation can sing along. Works such as the Handels' "Messiah" and the new "Young Messiah" are good to develop the voice and instrumental abilities so I encourage students to try some of these along with their chosen contemporary music.

Classical music requires the singer to be very disciplined in their singing. The breathing and diction are much more precise and the melody patterns are much harder to sing. A particular quality of sound is also required to present the song correctly which gives the student much opportunity to develop good tones and technical habits. When these are passed on into their contemporary music the quality is only enhanced and appreciated by the audience.

Some good examples of people who have applied these principles are; Sandi Patti, Steve Green, and Cliff Richard who has definitely stood the test of time.

PART FOUR

MOVEMENT NOTES FOR SINGERS & INSTRUMENTALISTS

CHOREOGRAPHY - DON'T JUST STAND THERE - DO SOMETHING!

So many times we see people in the church, doing "items", standing blank and lifeless as they're singing. It looks so boring as if they're wishing they were somewhere else! Both choirs, small groups, and solo songs can be enhanced by the use of designed choreographed steps. Youth choirs like to bounce to the beat of songs that they are singing. It is better to choreograph on up-tempo songs using unified movements, rather than have many different interpretations of body language, or standing like soldiers! Remember to look for "lips not hips" in all choreography especially up-tempo songs. Don't let the movement take away from the vocal understanding.

CHOIRS: should design their rows, so that everyone can be seen. A semi-circle is good. The use of "risers" or platforms can help with microphones and make good visual effects. In this way you can have up to six people around one microphone, as long as they learn to bend from the waist down to it.

SOLOISTS & GROUPS: can use positional choreographic movements which make the song relate to the audience both visually as well as audibly. So the message is portrayed to two senses, and gets imprinted in the memory of the congregation.

Learn to look at each other from time to time. Work out areas where you can all turn in the same direction or move forward for emphasis. Learn to hide mistakes and never let it show on your face. Look at different sections of the audience to include everyone and never look at the floor. Learn some basic dance steps and dramatic acting to help in expressing the meaning of the songs.

CHOREOGRAPHY

ALL MOVEMENTS;

1. Need to be done with *strength and control.*

2. *Be BIG* and definite so that the back row can see them.

3. Need to fit and enhance the words of the song.

4. Be very precise in timing.

5. The groups position design should portray the meaning of the song and attract attention of the audience.

6. Worship songs need very little movement, maybe arm raises.

7. Fast songs need quick, snappy and with definite moves.

8. Facial expressions are always important.

9. Always put yourself into the song and then deliver it from yourself to the audience to give it life and reality.

10. Remembering words and choreography takes concentration and much practice.

11. Work out where you need to move and how to vary it. Use hand gestures and change microphone from hand to hand sometimes in a song. In group numbers everyone is important. Guitarists must move a little, stepping forward or back sideways, always looking at others in the group as they sing.

SOLOISTS:
Some songs would be better sung sitting down in a more meditative devotional approach, either throughout the whole song or just part of it to create effect and atmosphere. Using a book can also add this devotional effect and help with hiding the words for the song! Always remember that words written or Sellotaped onto arms or hands will be seen by someone and become obvious as you refer to them. This is a very unprofessional approach! The best is always to memorize your words or have them on an overhead for the audience to see as well.

BEGINNINGS & ENDINGS:
These are always important and remembered by the audience.

   a. Beginnings; Face or Back to the audience? Head down and/or walk forward? Sitting or standing? Turn to sides?

   b. Endings; Turn to side? Head down? Step back? slight bow? Throw head back and hands up into the air? Turn your back? Run or walk off stage?

POINTS OF PERFORMANCE

1. **PRAYER**: Needed in every area, to be a cleansed vessel. Have the attitude of a servant. no "I"......

2. **PURPOSE**: What is your direction? and aim? To comfort, teach, evangelize, you need to know where you are heading.

3. **PROGRAM**: Co-ordinate it with your Purpose. Do music you can do well, and fits your vocal range. Are the lyrics good? Are they in line with your Purpose?

4. **PRACTICE:** Any good material needs much practice. Only add "little extras" if it enhances the song. Can you control the song?

5. **PERSONAL TESTIMONY:** Can you convey your testimony in speech as well as in song? Elements of a good testimony are: unique, Christ centred, personal, Bible based, clear and simple, positive, cliche free, up to date, fresh and new.

6. **PERSONAL APPEARANCE:** Be as tidy and neat as you can be. Make your body say the same as your mouth. Make your gestures the same as your words, not repetitive. Clothes; shirt sleeve, hems, colours, zips, snap fasteners, hair styles, and shoes.

7. **POSTURE:** Stand with one foot slightly behind the other in a "V" shape. Be upright and tall, not bent or crooked in any way. Sit with legs together and one slightly in front of the other ready to stand. Have hands resting in your lap or by your sides when standing.

8. **PRESENTATION/POISE**: Carry on no matter what happens! Speak calmly, "ad-lib" around situations, establish a rapport with the people. Can you be believable?

9. **PREPARATION**: Practice beforehand. Prepare yourself before you go on, emotionally, spiritually, physically. Perform to yourself in the mirror to check everything carefully.

STAGE INTRODUCTIONS

1. Make introductions short and precise. Decide beforehand what you are going to say and say no more.

2. Always look happy and pleased to meet them.

3. Stand and accept applause at the end with a smile.

4. Keep hands in one place; sides, or held together, unless you have something to do with them.

5. Think of the audience as an individual and look at the people. Don't always look at one space but look around, and imagine the people when the lights block them out.

6. Dress; plain colours and uncrushable materials are best. When on T.V, don't use whites, heavy patterns, spots or stripes.

7. Keep to songs of no more than three verses. Vary the type and tempo of the songs you sing also make sure they suit the occasion.

STAGE ENTRIES AND EXITS

1. *Prepare Yourself Beforehand*; in the side room off stage. Relax yourself by breathing deeply. Fresh oxygen helps quieten nerves Do three deep breaths in before entry. Hold the third breath and walk on feeling balanced by the "string" from the collar bone. Walk with behind in, tummy up, and gliding steadily with head held high naturally.

2. *SIT with foot forward* nearest to the next movement (right foot for the right and left for the left). *STAND* the same way. This gives balance and allows movement forward or backward without losing your balance or posture.

3. *SIT with hands* in lap one on top of the other lightly and relaxed, palms upwards. Stand up by leaning your body forward.

4. *BOW OF THANKS* if required, in formal occasions drop first the eyes, then head, then shoulders, and then come up gently. Be like a floppy doll. A Hand Gesture towards pianist is also required in formal occasions.

THE CHOIR & SMALL GROUP MEMBER

When you become a choir or small group member you take a place of spiritual leadership within the church. People will watch your lifestyle, especially the new Christians who will be taking their leading from you. Each member must be in tune with Christ to bring the group in tune with each other. In rehearsals and performances your total attention should be given to the music programme of the church.

THE AIM OF GROUP SINGING: The aim is to have a group of people singing together as one voice. The people become an instrument directed and played by the choir Director. As a choir member you should aim to blend your voice with the others and make a beautiful united pure sound that is pleasing to listen to. There is no room for a soloist in any group unless so directed by the leader! When you sing, your voice should be the same volume as the person next to you, no louder or softer, the "volume control" is adjusted by the Director.

ESSENTIALS FOR BEING A GOOD GROUP MEMBER:

1. *FAITHFULNESS:* Always be there, and ready.

2. *PUNCTUALITY*: Be on time, if not early, no excuses offered.

3. *APPROACH THE PLATFORM CAREFULLY:* Have a prayerful attitude with anticipation, excitement and appreciation. Group entrances should be carefully rehearsed.

4. *BE ALERT:* Always be ready to perform. Learn to be flexible in all situations, rarely does everything go exactly as rehearsed and planned.

5. *WATCH YOUR POSTURE*: Always stand and sit upright, no casualness and sloppy behaviour on the platform.

6. *BE ATTENTIVE:* No thumbing through the music, or writing notes, this is distracting to the audience and those around you. Be interested in all that is going on so that you don't miss your cue.

7. *WATCH THE DIRECTOR:* Always watch when singing, and keep the music out of sight of the audience.

8. *SING WITH A LOVE FOR SOULS:* If you as a group member love the souls of men and sing with this in mind, then love will show on your face.

9. *DEVELOP RESPONSIBILITY*: Towards the people and their needs. Romans 5 v 1 "We then that are strong ought to bear the infirmities of the weak and not to please ourselves".

10. *BE SUPPORTIVE:* Discover the difference between support and obligation. Philippians. 2 v 13. Support the director without criticism. If you can't stop murmuring and gossiping then you shouldn't be there.

11. *DEDICATE YOURSELF*: Have positive leadership attitudes.1 Timothy. 4 v 12
12. *VERBALIZE YOUR DREAMS*: Ask in faith and then you will receive the desires of your heart.

MINISTRY SONGS AND ITEMS

ITEMS

An Item is a song/dance/drama put into a service mainly to teach and entertain the congregation.
The subject matter does not necessarily have to be the same as the sermon, and several people can be involved.
Items should be arranged weeks in advance though often they are last minute "put togethers"! They are more frequently found in the evening services, especially when a guest speaker is present; but can be scheduled into the morning meetings. Usually Items are announced and placed before the sermon after the singing and announcements.
They take much preparation and practice and often the ministry value is not fully recognized by the Pastoral staff.

There are places for both Items and Ministry Songs and an understanding of the requirements for each is needed to be effective in the services.

MINISTRY SONGS

Ministry Songs are similar to Items but they have a specific purpose by the performers to minister to the congregation; to cause them to search their hearts and respond to the message in the song. The Pastoral staff should be aware of this and allow room for the ministry to take place. The placement of the song in the service is very important, and often the subject ties in with the sermon. Prayer ministry should be pre-arranged. Sometimes they are placed directly after the worship and not announced so as not to cut across the flow of the Holy Spirit in the worship. There can be more than one person involved; duets, trios, groups etc, but more often is just a solo. Sensitivity to what the Holy Spirit is wanting to do in the meeting, and continuity between the Pastoral staff and the person ministering in song is vital.

AUDITIONS, COMPETITIONS, TALENT QUESTS, & EXAMS

These things all take a great deal of preparation and cause stress. How do you deal with them? You need to be able to accept the comments and judgements that are handed out as part of the process of entering.
They are usually finished very quickly even though you spent hours over many days and weeks preparing your songs.

Do not be shy but be confident as you walk in and stand correctly.
2 Timothy 1 v 7 *"For God did not give us a spirit of timidity, but a spirit of power, of love and of self-discipline."*

Be prepared for anything that may be given you to do. Your performance techniques will be judged here as well as your ability.

In Exams, make sure you can sight read written music and do "ear tests". Have your teacher train you in these things beforehand. Know your vocal range and favourite songs. Do not be upset if they stop you before your song is finished and say nothing! Auditions and Exams are quite ruthless and your feelings come off second best. They often have a fixed time limit. Examiners are not allowed to talk to you particularly in classical exams which are very formal and serious occasions. You could need at least six months of preparation doing set songs to pass a vocal classical exam.

When choosing a song for an Audition or Competition, choose one that is;
a, Not too long.
b, Is definitely in the correct key for your voice.
c, Has a good range of notes.
d, Is of a suitable style for the occasion.

Learn the song thoroughly and don't change anything at the last minute. The more you have practiced and memorised the words the less likely you are to blank out when the nerves hit you. Two or three months of work on a song is required for these occasions, not just two or three weeks!

While you are waiting, keep as calm as you can by praying. Stay away from others that get nervous as they may cause you to panic! You must keep yourself as steady as possible so that your brain can function quickly. Shut yourself in the toilets if necessary! Eat a little energy food no closer than half an hour before your performance. Stay away from anything spicy or repeatable! Dress well and choose something appropriate for the occasion. Organise everything ahead of time, so that last minute panics with ties, colours, hair do's and make up are avoided.

Be careful who you have around you the day before the event. Have no one who is going to upset you emotionally. Seek out people that are encouraging and have confidence in you and what you are doing. You need a good support team! Someone who is there afterwards to help calm you down and take your mind off things. Have an event planned to go to afterwards to help you deprogram yourself.

Singing is a personal thing and you can be emotionally hurt if you do not do as well as you expected. Know that God still loves you and the world has not stopped! Life goes on and so must you. Sometimes we are our own worst enemy so a post-mortem is not a good idea. They can tear apart and destroy your self-confidence more than the actual comments given by the examiners/auditioners! Be aware of your own limitations and expectations.

PART FIVE

SOUND TECHNIQUES

SOUND PRODUCTION

VIBRATIONS;

1. To make a sound you must first make a vibration. All sound is caused by vibration such as the loudspeaker in a stereo or your vocal cords. You can sometimes see or feel sound vibrations. Try this by touching your throat as you speak or sing, or watch the piano strings as you press the keys.

2. Anything that vibrates regularly produces a note - musical sound. Irregular vibrations cause noise. Anything vibrating at 261 times per second produces the note of "middle C". Faster vibrations produce higher notes and slower vibrations lower notes.

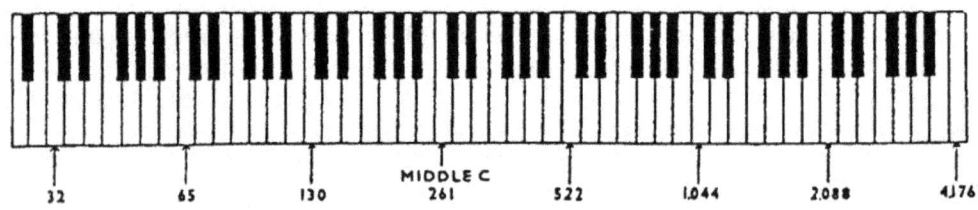

These vibrations per second are approximate.

3. In instruments that produce sounds from vibrating strings, the "pitch" of the note depends on three things; the length, the tension, and the thickness of the string.

4. The highness or lowness of a note is called its PITCH.

5. In woodwind instruments, the air inside the tube is made to vibrate. A long column of air vibrates more slowly than a short column. Remember the slower the vibration the lower the note.

6. The loudness or softness of a note depends upon the strength of the vibrations that caused it. In most instruments the part that vibrates would not produce enough sound on its own, so the body of the instrument acts as a resonator and works like an amplifier. When using your voice, the spaces in your mouth and head give the vibrations resonance and can make your voice sound louder.

7. When we hear a single note we also hear other notes coming forth called overtones or harmonics. The mixture of overtones gives us the tone colour of an instrument (voice). A

sound with a lot of overtones will sound bright and with less overtones it will sound more mellow.

8. A pure note with no harmonics is called a fundamental. Harmonics are multiples of a fundamental note. Every note on a normal musical instrument consists not of a "pure" tone like that of a tuning-fork, but of a blend of the "fundamental" and certain upper harmonics the precise blend differing between instruments. This difference in blend determines the difference between tone-colours of instruments or voices. For example, the sound of a saxophone differs to that of a flute due to the harmonics involved. This is the same with younger voices compared with more mature voices and may be easier to notice when listening to sopranos.

The whole length vibrates, and so do the two halves, and the three thirds

Several sections are therefor vibrating at the same time

SOUND SYSTEMS

Most Churches and auditoriums these days use a sound system of one sort or another. The four basic components found in all systems are; Microphones, Cables, Amplifier and Speakers.
A sound system may also have other components to enhance the sound such as reverb/delay, compression or a de-esser. Foldback is another handy extra you might come across.
Some of these terms may be unfamiliar to you so I will try and explain them to you.

Reverb or Delay. This is the effect that can be added to your voice or instrument to make it sound as though you were in a large empty hall. It's not really an echo where the words are repeated but adds more of a depth to your voice. Some churches have a natural resonance that causes this effect due to the physical size of the building. The wall coverings have an effect on this as well. A room with a lot of people or with carpeted walls, tends to soak up sound and this is where a reverb unit would be most beneficial.

A *compressor* is used to limit the level of a sound so that everything is at roughly at the same volume. This is particularly handy if you plan to broadcast the sound over a radio station or TV.

A *de-esser* is a device that cuts out certain frequencies over 10 000 Hertz limiting the effective sibilence of your voice. Confused? Sibilence is a term used to describe the clarity of your voice with regard to how much emphasis you place on words with an "S" sound. Some people have an exessive sibilence and when put through a sound system will sound very "essey" on words like "this".

Foldback. This is not the same as Feedback. Foldback is best descibed as a parallel sound system that runs in conjunction with the main sound system. Its purpose is to allow the people performing or on stage to hear themselves. There are special floor speakers or monitors that are pointed at the performers for this purpose.

Feedback is the effect where sound coming out of the speakers is picked up by the microphones and re-amplified. This then comes out of the speakers at a louder level and more gets into the microphones causing a cycle to occur. This happens very fast and if not stopped, it may destroy the speakers and your hearing. The best way to stop this happening is to turn down the volume on the sound board.

The diagram below is that of a sound board. It has a number of duplicate channels starting with 1 on the left and going up to 24 or more on the right. The microphones are plugged in at the top of the board on the left hand side while the speakers or amplifier feeds are plugged in on the right hand side. Most of the knobs on the board are to do with volume or tone. Generally the knobs at the bottom labelled 1 to 24 are individual volume adjustments. There are usually 2 to 4 controls on the bottom right hand side of the board which are the master control volumes.

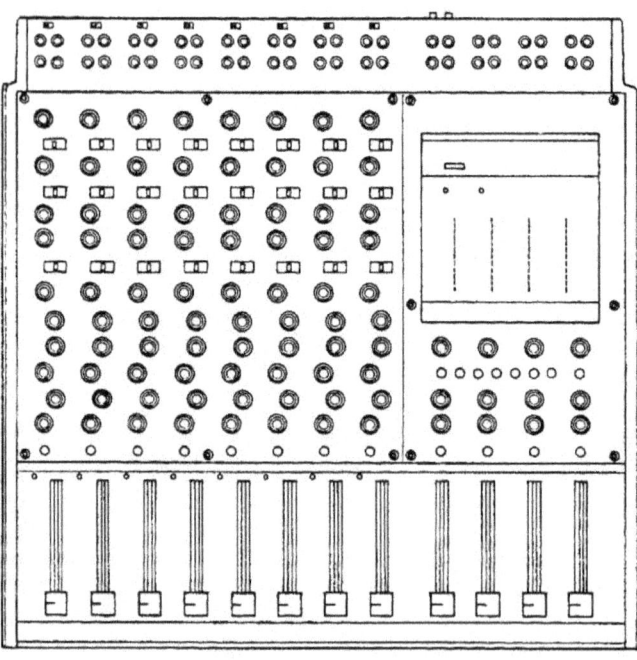

MICROPHONE TECHNIQUES

Hold the microphone lightly yet firmly. Keep it at least a few inches distance away from your mouth allowing people to see the movement of your lips and your mouth shapes. The microphone must move with your body and head and stay the same distance from your mouth. It is good to bring the microphone closer to your mouth for notes that you are a little weak on such as low notes for a soprano, and further away on your really strong notes.

The way a microphone works is by picking up the sound vibrations that are generated by your voice and turning them into electrical signals. These electrical signals travel down the microphone lead and are picked up by the amplifier on the other end. This is the opposite to a loud speaker which converts electrical signals into the audio signals that we can hear.

There are quite a few different types of microphone available and most people only get to see or use 2 or 3 of these.

A *Carbon* microphone is used in older style telephones. They don't have a very good frequency response, which means they don't pick up low and high frequencies very well.

A *Moving Coil or Dynamic* microphone is the most common type used today. It has a good frequency response and is sensitive enough for most purposes. Their main disadvantage is that they can't be made very small so usually they are made in the form of a hand held unit. The way it works is, a coil of fine copper wire is wound on a thin plastic membrane which in turn is housed between two magnets. When the plastic membrane vibrates in sympathy with the voice vibrations, there is an electric current generated in the copper coil. The amplifier can then recognise these electrical impulses and amplify them as required.

A *Ribbon* microphone is very directional and delicate. Some "Shotgun" microphones use ribbons to pick up sound.

A *Shotgun* microphone has a specific purpose and that is to pick up sounds from a long distance. They get the name Shotgun because of their very directional nature. You sometimes see them used by a T.V. crew when they want to pick up a reporters voice and not show the microphone on T.V. (they are the long fluffy microphones!).

A *Condenser* microphone is the second most common type of microphone and is generally used in Tie-pin microphones where space is at a premium. They can be made very small. The way these microphones work is by use of a fixed conducting back plane with a thin diaphragm in front. As the sound pressure hits this diaphragm it allows it to vibrate. This movement changes the capacitance of the microphone and this is what the Amplifier picks up.

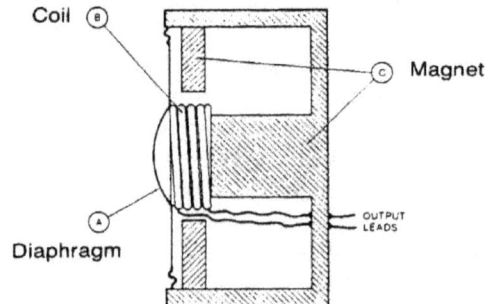

MOVING COIL OR DYNAMIC MICROPHONE

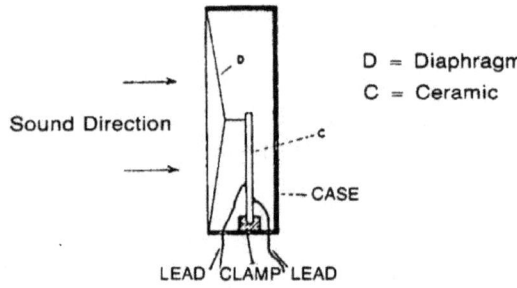

ONE FORM OF CONSTRUCTION OF CRYSTAL MICROPHONE

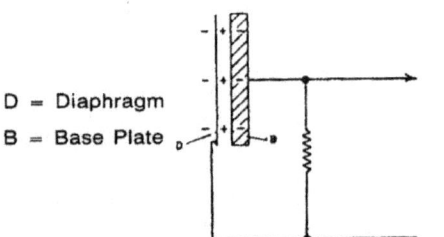

PRINCIPLE OF ELECTRET MICROPHONE

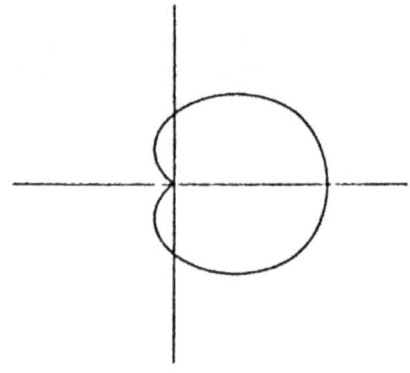

POLAR DIAGRAM OF CARDIOID MICROPHONE

Microphones are available with generally two types of response; the Cardioid and the Omni. The Cardioid picks up sound mainly from the front and is not very suitable if 2 or more people are using the same microphone. The Omni picks up sound from in front as well as the sides. Microphones are very delicate and expensive so it pays to be gentle with them and take care of them well. The best way to check if a microphone is turned on is to talk into it or click your fingers. You can easily ruin a microphone by blowing into it, or by tapping it. Microphones like these generally cost around $400 to $500 so treat them with respect.

PART SIX

CHURCH INSTRUMENTALISTS

A MUSICIANS PRAYER

By faith in your Word, Lord Jesus, I am a creative skilful musician. Therefore I believe and receive that in the natural I am becoming a highly skilful musician, and that in the spiritual I am developing wisdom, ability, and power from God Almighty. When I minister in music, people will be refreshed, healed and delivered. Even difficult cases like Saul shall be set free. Everything that was Davids' in his miraculous music ministry I claim as mine, as a born again, spirit filled Christian, and so much more, Lord Jesus.

THE CHIEF MUSICIAN - WORSHIP DIRECTOR

1. *His purpose*;
It is to oversee the music, and musicians; ie the singers, instrumentalists, worship leaders, outreach music and youth music.

2. *Qualities of the Chief Musician;*

   1. A good grounding in the Word,
   2. Leadership abilities,
   3. Strength of character,
   4. Faithfulness,
   5. Authority,
   6. Compassion for people,
   7. An organized ability,
   8. Understanding of music theory,
   9. Prayerful understanding of the musicians,
   10. A love and ability to gather the people.

THE PURPOSES OF INSTRUMENTS IN CHURCH

1. To minister to God in His presence. 1 Chronicles 16 v 4,6 & 37. *"...The priests were to blow the trumpets regularly..."*

2. To Praise God. 1 Chronicles 23 v 5 *"...Four thousand are to praise the Lord with the musical instruments I have provided for that purpose."* Psalm 33 v 2, Psalm 71 v 22. Psalm 91 v 1 to 3. Psalm 98 v 5 & 6, Psalm 149 v 3, Psalm 150 v 3 to 5.

3. To accompany singers in joy and praise. Psalm 81 v 1.
1 Chronicles 15 v 16, *"...To appoint their brothers as singers to sing joyful songs, accompanied by musical instruments: lyers, harps and cymbals."*

4. To call and lead in Worship. Psalm 81 v 3, Psalm 92 v 1 to 3, Numbers 10 v 2 *"Make two trumpets of hammered silver, and use them for calling the community together and for having the camps set out."*

5. To prepare for prophecy. 1 Samuel 10 v 5, 2 Kings 3 v 15,
"...Bring me a harpist. While the harpist was playing, the hand of the Lord came upon Elisha..."

6. To lead and play in warfare. Numbers 10 v 2 to 10, Psalm 144 v 1 *"Praise be to the Lord my rock, who trains my hands for war, my fingers for battle."*

7. To usher in and declare God's presence. Psalm 47 v 5 *"God has ascended amid shouts of joy, the Lord amid the sounding of trumpets."*

8. To teach the Nations to Praise.

MINISTERING TO THE LORD ON THE INSTRUMENTS;

In order for our music to bring glory to Jesus, and be effective as a tool for ministry, we need to seek Him first in everything. We need to study His Word, in relation to music, and ask for the anointing of the Holy Spirit upon our lives.

1. Isaiah. 10 v 27 *"The yoke shall be destroyed because of the anointing."* To anoint means to smear or rub with oil for the purpose of consecration. Dedicated to the service or worship of God. In the Old Testament priests were anointed and set apart for God service.
See also Exodus 28 v 41; 40 v 15.
It would be good to have a Minister pray for you and your instrument or voice and set you apart for ministry when you know for sure you have been called. If you seek God seriously you will eventually know if you are called for this ministry.

2. 1 Samuel 16 v 13. *"So Samuel took the horn of oil and anointed him in the presence of his brothers, and from that day on the Spirit of the Lord came upon David in power..."*

David's ministry was anointed and prayed for by Samuel. David was also skillful, he practised! 1 Samuel 16 v 17 *"So Saul said to his attendants, find someone who plays well and bring him to me."*
David's music brought deliverance 1 Samuel 16 v 23.

3. Psalm 33 v 2 & 3 *"Praise the Lord with the harp, sing unto Him with the Psaltery and an instrument of ten strings. Sing to him a new song; play skillfully, and shout for joy."*

1. Sing unto Him a new song. The Hebrew word is YATAB which means to be or make well, literally sound beautiful.

2. Play skilfully with a loud noise. The Hebrew word here is ZAMAR which means, to strike with the fingers; to touch the strings or parts of a musical instrument, ie to play upon it to make music.

4. The Minstrel's anointing.
2 Kings 3 v 15 *"But now bring me a harpist. While the harpist was playing, the hand of the Lord came upon Elisha"* (prophet).
The Minstrels Anointing was often an anointed music ministry which releases the prophetic ministry. A minstrel was a wandering singer who sang songs of his own composing, to the accompaniment of a harp. A poet, a singer or a musician. The word is related to "minister" or a "servant", one who gives help.

5. Prophesying on the Instruments;
1 Chronicles 25 v 1 *"...David set apart some of the sons of Asaph, Heman and Jeduthun for the ministry of prophesying, accompanied by harps, lyres and cymbals."*
The musician priests that David appointed for service in the house of the Lord were to prophecy on their instruments. As New Testament priests, we are to stir up the gifts of God for the building up of the church. 1 Corinthians 14 v 1,3 & 26 *"Desire spiritual gifts... when you come together every one of you hath a psalm, doctrine, tongue, revelation, interpretation. Let all things be done unto edifying."*

We minister unto the Lord by being faithful in our technical studies, ie practice, as well as spending time worshipping him freely on the instrument. Isaiah 61 v 1 & 3.

SINGING IN THE SPIRIT or FREE PRAISE & WORSHIP

WHAT IS IT?

This is a form of Worship that is found mostly in Reformed churches. It is allowing the Holy Spirit freedom to express worship through the use of your voice. Worship initiated by the Holy Spirit is God inspired and anointed.
Ephesians 5 v 19 *"... addressing one another with Psalms, Hymns, and Spiritual songs, singing and making melody in your hearts to the Lord."*

God desires our worship, and will help us give the freedom of expression needed for the Holy Spirit to sing through us.
Romans 8 v 26 *"...the Spirit helps our weaknesses...v 27 ...intercedes for us according to the will of God."* This is true in prayer as well as in praise and worship.

John 4 v 23 *"True worshippers will worship the Father in spirit and truth." v 24 "God is spirit and those who worship Him must worship in spirit and in truth."*

HOW DO YOU DO IT?

The key to this form of worship is allowing freedom of expression of the Holy Spirit within you to come out. Allow whatever notes and words that are inside you to come out. Usually it is easiest to flow along with the music being played during the time of worship, or after a song is played or sung.

The last notes and chords of the music gives the key to start on. The pianist leading in a simple chord progression moving from the last chord of a song helps greatly.

CHORD PATTERNS

The song "Holy Spirit let your presence fall" ends on a "C". Try this chord sequence;

C - Am - Dm7 - G - C and then repeat the pattern,
(chord I - VImin - IImin7 - V - I).

For songs ending in G, a good pattern is;

G - Em - C - D - G.
(chord I - VImin - IV - V - I).

You can just go from the C to the G (chord I & V) for a simple start and then add to it once the congregation has become used to it.

It is a good idea to hum or ah those notes and then just sing in your own language any praise words that come to mind, and switch over to your tongue language when led, if you have this gift.

Free Worship is an emotional thing, worship does involve your feelings because you need to use them to express praise and adoration, love, joy, and sadness to God.

God does have and understand feelings, and using different volumes can add to your expression which brings beneficial release of the Holy Spirit through you.

THE HEBREW WORDS FOR PRAISE

BARAK: kneel, bless, salute, praise. Judges 5 v 2, Psalm 72 v 15 *"...and daily shall he be praised."* This refers to a kind of silence, no statement of vocal expressions.

YADAH: Thankful expression of praise. Throw hands forward or upwards in confession. 2 Chronicles 20 v 21,
Psalm 9 v 1 *"I will praise you O Lord with all my heart."*
Psalm 28 v 7, 43 v 4 & 5, 111 v 1, 138 v 1, 2 & 4. A heart felt praise with outward sign of lifted hands. Describing a lifted heart, a powerful act of praise.

TOWDAH: Thanksgiving and praise for what God is going to do. The sacrifice of praise, and lifted hands implied faith praise.
Psalm 42 v 4, 50 v 23, 56 v 12, Isaiah 51 v 3.

ZAMAR: Instrumental and sung praise, meaning to touch the strings. Psalm 21 v 13 *"Be exalted, O Lord, in your strength; we will sing and praise your might."*
Psalm 149 v 3 *"Let them praise His name with dancing and make music to Him with tambourine and harp."*
Psalm 57 v 7 *"My heart is steadfast, I will sing and make music."*

SHABACH: To triumph, glory, shout, address in a loud tone, God sanctions this volume of praise.
Psalm 63 v 3 & 4, 117 v 1, 145 v 4, 147 v 12.

SHEBACH: To give praise. Daniel 2 v 23 *"I thank and praise you O God of my fathers..."*, 4 v 34 *"At the end of that time, I, Nebuchadnezzar raised my eyes toward heaven, and my sanity was restored. Then I praised the MOST HIGH; I honoured and glorified Him who lives forever."*

AINEO: To praise. Luke 2 v 13 & 20, 19 v 37, 24 v 53, Acts 2 v 47, 3 v 8 & 9, Romans 15 v 11.
Revelation 19 v 5 *"Then the voice came from the thrown saying Praise our God all you his servants, you who fear him both small and great."*

HALAL: Halleluliah, to shine, boast, celebrate, commend, sing, rave, be clamorously foolish. Most common word in scripture!
2 Chronicles 31 v 2, 20 v 19 *"Then some Levites stood up and praised the Lord, the God of Israel, with a very loud voice."*
Ezra 3 v 10 & 11 *"...and all the people gave a great shout of praise to the Lord, because the foundation of the house of the Lord was laid."*
1 Chronicles 23 v 5 & 30, Nehemiah 5 v 13, 12 v 24, Psalm 22 v 22, 23 & 26, 35 v 18, 56 v 4 & 10, 63 v 5, 69 v 30 & 34, Psalm 74 v 21, 107 v 32, 109 v 30, 119 v 164 & 175.

TEHILLAH: High praise to sing and glorify. Exodus 15 v 11,
2 Chronicles 20 v 22, Psalm 22 v 3 & 25, 33 v 1, 34 v 1, 35 v 28, 40 v 3, 65 v 1, 71 v 6, 8 & 14, 78 v 4, 79 v 13, 102 v 21, 106 v 2, 12 & 47, 109 v 1, 119 v 171, 145 all, 148 v 14, 149 v 1, Isaiah 42 v 8, 10 & 12, 61 v 3 & 11. This differs from the rest as it implies that God has responded to the praises of his people which means God inhabits and is enthroned in the midst of the praise. God is a consuming fire requiring reverence.
Jeremiah 13 v 11, 17 v 14, 33 v 9, 48 v 2, 51 v 41, Habakkuk 3 v 3, Zephaniah 3 v 19 & 20.

SHACACH: To bow down, prostrate oneself to fall flat, to reverence, to fall on knees with forehead touching the ground.

PROSKUNEO: As a dog would lick the hand of his master, worship is our response to Him once He has manifested Himself in our midst.

PART SEVEN:

WORSHIP

WORSHIP PREREQUISITES;

1. You must have a desire to worship. Prepare your heart, no flesh will prevail.
2. Be tender hearted desiring after spiritual things.
Romans 8 v 5 to 13.
3. A major hindrance is unreconciled relationships.
Matthew 5 v 23 to 25.

FACTORS TO ATTAINING WORSHIP;

1. Boundless confidence; or trust in God. Jeremiah 32 v 17, Psalm 91, 1 Peter 5 v 7.
2. Admiration; a delighted and pleased attitude of approval
3. Fascination; with His presence, be filled with excitement and captivated with the presence of God.
4. Adoration; A love, devotion, and respect towards God.

Worship is not a human invention but a divine offer in a personal relationship. He responds to our efforts towards Him. True worship effects every part of your being.

HINDRANCES TO WORSHIP;

1. Devil and demons resist Praise and Worship.
2. Changing of Bible concepts eg; worship changed to reverence, a shout changed to silence, a clap changed to clasp of preachers hand, freedom changed to formality.
3. Generally there is a reduced image of God's work today.
4. Fear of man.
5. Pride and Rebellion.
6. Controlled by our senses instead of the Word of God.
7. Failure to understand worship's preparation function, for revelation, teaching, and the gifts. Praise prepares you for teaching.
8. Failure to recognize the influence of worship upon faith.
9. Failure to perceive worship's protective power.
10. Living an undedicated life.

WHAT HAPPENS WHEN WE WORSHIP

Worship is our response to the presence of God. The more we worship the more the presence of God becomes real to us and we change into God's likeness.

Man was created by God to worship Him; to have communion with Him. For man to worship his creator would be his most fulfilling function.

Man has a need within himself to love and is made to be the companion of God. Even when man fell (first sinned), God provided a way to redeem him so that he could still fulfil his primary function and have the close relationship with his creator.

Man has to learn to supress his will and selfish nature, and develop the constant love and obedience required to worship God in true holiness and commitment. The gospel of John tells us in Chapter 6 v 23 & 24. *"True worshippers will worship the Father in Spirit and truth, for such the Father seeks to worship Him."* To do this the love of Christ must firstly be in us by the Salvation experience, as man cannot worship God if he doesn't know him personally. Then a progressive experience of learning and living with God allows him to surrender his life and come into a more loving and deeper relationship with his creator.

Worship requires man to surrender himself to Christ, and in doing so, become more like He is; having His nature worked into us by being in His presence. That which we adhere to, we become a part of, and take on its likeness be it good or evil.
The children of Israel were perfect examples to us of what happens when we worship God and when we worship idols.

God commanded them to worship no other Gods before Him in Exodus 20, when He gave the Ten Commandments. He promised them blessing and prosperity as long as they adhered to His statutes and worshipped only their creator. Many instructions were given, how to do things and perform all God's requirements, but the children of Israel like us, murmured and disobeyed, showing a heart that was not totally committed to God, and so God had to teach them how to live a committed obedient life to be true worshippers.

In Exodus 32 the children of Israel decided to go their own way and began to worship an idol. They disobeyed and did not trust God. These requirements are built into every true worshipper as they move into a closer walk with their God. God was merciful to these people many times and sought to teach them how to love him. God longed for the love and fellowship of His people. So God renewed His covenant with them in Exodus 34; and continued to teach His people of His purposes for them.

When we worship we become more and more closer to the one we worship, and form a bond or covenant with them. It is a two way relationship that grows as time is spent together. A bond of love, trust and obedience required by man to relate to His God. Man develops a submissive attitude and a deep constant love commitment to the one who created him.

God's purposes are not just for this world, but are much more far reaching so the quicker we learn the lessons here in this space of time, the better and more prepared we will be when we go to be with Him in Glory.

The more time we spend in the presence of God the more we will become like Him. God wants us to worship Him and be changed more and more so that we may serve Him better in the eternal days to come.

THE SONG AND WORSHIP LEADER

Christian Worship defies definition, but must be experienced to be known. It is a spontaneous encounter with God requiring sensitivity to the voice of the Lord by the worshipper's spirit. A direct acknowledgement of who God is.

Worship is not mechanical and there is no formula to be used. Worship is used to give physical expression to what is going on inside your spirit. Worship acknowledges God's supremacy and results in your realization of your insufficiency. Submission acknowledges God's sovereign right to a persons life and dedicates that life to God.

1. There are three parts to Worship;
    A. To feel specifically in your heart. Mark 5 v 29, Acts 28 v 3.
    B. To express in some way in the body, your feelings.
    C. Humility. Isaiah 6 v 1 to 5.

2. Practical Aspects to Leading Worship;
    A. Song List needed with keys listed and sometimes with a Theme. Introduce only one new song at a time.
    B. Anticipate the words to lead the group, you need to be ahead of them to lead them.
    C. Use familiar songs and maintain the tempo keeping it strong and solid. Drummer and Bass player need to be controlled and led by the Spirit.
    D. You need a system of hand signals for the instrumentalists.
    E. Know your key signatures for the songs.

3. Be confident and prepared in Christ.

4. Appearance;

    Church group size of 1 to 100 blend in
    Church group size of 100 to 500 be neat
    Church group size of 500 to 5000 stand out

Be well groomed, with modest dress and no tight fitting or revealing clothing. Ladies remember the stage is well lit so wear a slip under light coloured or thin clothing. Men singing on stage must wear a dress jacket and tie. During the week a tie is not essential but still the jacket is preferred.

5. Song Selection;

    Church group size of 1 to 100 follow the Spirit
    Church group size of 100 to 500 confirm the Spirit
    Church group size of 500 to 5000 reveal the Spirit

Memorize your words and / or music, be spiritually prepared by spending some quality time in prayer before the service. Have accompaniments arranged at least two weeks ahead of time and NO rock (heavy beat) songs on Sunday unless authorized.
Choose songs that are "word" oriented and that minister - victory faith type songs that edify and encourage. Get sound levels for Special Music at least one week before the day of singing so make arrangements with Sound Technician.

6. Spiritual Authority:

    Church groups size of 1 to 100 let the Holy Spirit establish authority
    Church groups size of 100 to 500 your authority must be recognized
    Church groups size of 500 to 5000 demonstrate your authority

7. Delivery;

Learn to flow with the Holy Spirit and have no unnecessary delays. Just sing or play and don't preach or teach which includes no lengthy testimonials. Anointing is more important than "professionalism".

8. Execution;

    Church groups size of 1 to 100 inward confidence & outward submission
    Church groups size of 100 to 500 inward authority & outward confidence
    Church groups size of 500 to 5000 inward victory & outward authority

    8a) Start with Strength;
    Church groups size of 1 to 100 spiritual strength
    Church groups size of 100 to 500 verbal strength
    Church groups size of 500 to 5000 demonstrate strength

8b) Make Service Connected;
Church groups size of 1 to 100 follow the Holy Spirit
Church groups size of 100 to 500 predetermine the Holy Spirit
Church groups size of 500 to 5000 plan the service in prayer

8c) Get the Attention of the People;
Church groups size of 1 to 100 let Jesus be seen
Church groups size of 100 to 500 ask question for verbal response
Church groups size of 500 to 5000 give direction requiring Action

9. Direction;

Church groups size of 1 to 100 rely on the Holy Spirit
Church groups size of 100 to 500 build from natural to spiritual
Church groups size of 500 to 5000 start big in soul realm, move to quietness in worship

10. Directing;

Church groups size of 1 to 100 instrument carries rhythm
Church groups size of 100 to 500 song leader starts rhythm instruments
Church groups size of 500 to 5000 song leader does big directing

10a) Words;
Church groups size of 1 to 100 sing out
Church groups size of 100 to 500 use microphone
Church groups size of 500 to 5000 direct words & be slightly ahead

10b) Dramatize spiritual nature;
Church groups size of 1 to 100 sing with all your heart
Church groups size of 100 to 500 verbally direct attention to spirit
Church groups size of 500 to 5000 dynamically exhort people to Worship.

"SING UNTO HIM" Psalm 105 v 1 & 2.

PART EIGHT:

FREQUENTLY ASKED QUESTIONS;

Why should I take Singing Lessons?

I've been selected to sing on the church worship team, so I must have a good voice. Do I really need lessons?
The parable of the talents in Matthew 25: 14 - 30 contains many lessons for us to learn from and holds the answers to some of these questions. The principle is that whatever deposit of ability God has given you He expects you to use and develop. So whether you consider yourself to have a great voice or just be able to make it in the music team, God expects you to be a good servant not only to use your gift but also to increase and develop the talent given you.

Will it change my natural style? I don't want to sound like an opera singer.

The techniques of how to sing correctly are the same for any style of voice a person chooses to have. If you work on the foundation principles to produce correct sounds, then styles can be developed later. It pays to select your teacher wisely because they will only teach out of what they know.

What do you do in a lesson, just sing songs?

Lessons are designed to help a person retrain the brain to do things correctly. This is particularly true after spending your life producing sounds by copying others and unknowingly developing incorrect habits. It takes time to teach new habits and so exercises are used to teach the correct principles, which will eventually be applied into songs that you sing.

The older people ask me; "Am I too old to learn to sing or do the Theory?"

I sometimes get a call from some older ladies that have finished working and would like to be involved more with their singing. I have learnt that there is a place for all ages in music ministry in churches. With God you are not too old to learn and develop your gifts. The colour of your hair does not dictate the abilities that you have!

Why should I learn music theory?

A knowledge of music theory adds logical reasoning and develops abstract thinking. The student learns that music is not a haphazard collection of notes and sounds but is an orderly arrangement of rules. Learning the principles of music theory brings a higher level of musical understanding, giving insight into composition, an aid to memorisation of music and appreciation of the historical composers. Musicians that play by ear sometimes use this ability as an excuse not to learn how to read music. Aural training usually convinces people how vague their initial impressions are and how temporary the results can be. Songwriter's find that they can forget easily what they create and a lack of written knowledge a real disadvantage when producing new material.

At what age can my child have singing lessons?

I have found that usually it is around the age of six years, as soon as a child is able to sit still and concentrate for about half an hour, they are ready to begin lessons. Before this time the parents can encourage and develop music appreciation and rhythm by doing things at home.

At what age can my child learn how to read the music?

There are some great teaching materials available for young children to begin reading and writing the musical notation. Special books are written for different ages from 4 years up.
How can I tell if my child has some musical talent to sing or play an instrument?
The parents can try playing music and observing the child's sense of rhythm and vocal ability. Some children's voices do not tune up until around 6 years others earlier. I think it is a good policy to just to try the child with something that they show an interest in and see how the lessons develop.

Should children be allowed to be on the singing teams at church?

Many churches have large music teams but how many include children. It seems that they are not considered often but I think if the child has been serious with their learning and understands what is involved then why not have them helping with the music. They often can sing better than some of the adults!

Should a Song Leader be able to sing in Tune?

Generally it is always much better to be able to sing in tune if you want good flowing worship. There is the general thought that if a Song Leader has good back up singers they don't have to be good at singing themselves. I have found it to be a great disadvantage if the song leader cannot find the start notes and first phrases to a song because the initial start note leads the congregation and keeps the flow of worship. The Singers, Instrumentalists and congregation all should take their leads from the song leader; so if he cannot begin correctly it can all fall apart. The soundman can turn the song leader down if the sound is leading the congregation astray, but he can only do so much with a voice! In small church situations this becomes even more critical especially when teaching a new song.

Should a Music Director be able to sing in tune?

Not really because a Music Director does not necessarily have to be a Song Leader, especially if they are more gifted in the instrumental area rather than singing. It is always good for a Music Director to be willing to acknowledge their weaknesses by have assistants in the areas where they are not so gifted. This helps to develop team work and prevents a controlling situation in the team. It can bring involvement within the group and gives a sense of responsibility and commitment. In small churches where there is not the availability of people one should try to work with what is there. In your eagerness to be up with the latest in worship it is easy to go beyond the talent present. Try to guard against people trying to do things that they are not gifted for thus moving out of their ministries, this only leads to frustrations within the team members and lack of anointing in the worship.

Generally if you find yourself in the position of Song Leader or Music Director it would pay you to seek lessons in the areas of weakness that you may have. The Lord expects us to use and develop our talents to the best we can. Read the parable of the Talents found in Matthew 25 verses 14 to 30. Do not limit your usefulness to God by lack of knowledge and ability. If you can play only by ear learn also how to read written music, and if you are better at playing than singing then try to learn the basics of singing. Doing this will broaden your understanding of the whole music ministry. Always minister in the strong areas where you know God has called you to, and teach yourself in the weak areas. These things can take years to develop so be patient as you learn.

Why have I been moved out of the singing team at church?

When it comes to the selection of people on the music teams at church, it is sad to say that sometimes there is prejudice against age. Yes it does happen and I think the younger music directors fail to see the value in age and experience that "grey or white power" can bring!. The type of music used should not dictate the age of the singer or player. There is a trend going around to change to modern bands and younger people excluding the older people. I have found that some older people like the modern music and the hymns contain deep truths that have lasted much longer than the current choruses. It is worth remembering that the anointing of the Holy Spirit is not governed by the age of something. God loves variety and there should be a balance in all things**.**

Should an obviously pregnant lady be seen up front in the music team?

This is a personal choice; but I would not recommend being in such a public and obvious position. It could distract people in the congregation from worship, to see a largely pregnant lady, and if anything should happen to her during that time it would be embarrassing to everyone! Remembering that she is still a person and quite capable of doing things, the lady can always sing sitting down, but upright, in the front row with a microphone. In this way she is still made to feel welcome and not isolated from the team.

Will being pregnant effect my breathing and singing quality?

YES. This seems to effect everyone at some stage be it early or later on as the baby takes up more room and stretches the abdominal muscles. The diaphragm needs room to move and abdominal muscles need to be strong, so if they are also working to hold a baby and being stretched in the process then they will not be able to support the notes as well. There will be lack of strength to produce the sound, and the body could also lack energy, so the quality and quantity will be effected. As the baby moves down in later pregnancy the lady may find that she can sing a little better than before, as the pressure is taken off the diaphragm. After the birth the lady should work hard at getting the muscles strong again, if she is serious about her singing ministry. There is no easy way around this except to say that the more stretching you have endured the more work is needed to tighten the muscles! So several babies mean more work! The abdominal muscles are very important for singing and need to be well maintained throughout your ministry. Do the exercises given you by the physiotherapist and go to a gym and get the body strong again to do what the Lord has called you to. " Flabby tummy muscles means a flabby voice "!

I have had ladies ask me "Should I have singing lessons while I am pregnant"?

I have found that it depends upon the person concerned. Some ladies have an easy time and are quite fit while others find that things like morning sickness and other adjustments seem to bother them and cause lifestyle upsets. The first six months or so can be quite easy and then as the baby gets bigger the lady may find it harder to breathe and sing well. This may be the time to stop for a season and resume later on.

Should I sing or preach if I have a cold?

It depends upon what stage the cold is at. If the throat area is at all infected then the answer is no, because it could cause more damage to the larynx and vocal chords. If it is in the head area then you can still sing quite well and can sometimes sound richer than before! If the nose is dripping then take something to dry it up but with caution. Sometimes the medicine can also dry up the throat area, which would make it sore especially if you use it to preach or sing.

Should I sing or preach if I have a sore throat?

If your voice is affected and sounds croaky no. If it sounds OK, and doesn't hurt to speak then you maybe able to gently, but it would be wise to be careful. Avoid using throat lozenges that have anaesthetic in them as it can numb the throat and you may not be aware of any damage you may be doing to it.

What can I do to guard against colds, flu', and infections?

Generally you need to be fit and healthy and have a good diet. The body needs to be able to fight off any germs that come your way and needs to be in good condition to do this. If you find you are susceptible to this sort of illness, a flu' vaccine may be worth considering. A sensible form of dress will also help through the winter.

Why do I get a sore throat, or loose my voice, after song leading or preaching?

If your voice feels tight or tired afterwards and maybe a little lower in pitch; it is just a case of over use and will usually get better after rest. The constant long use at a louder volume has over worked the area. Preaching at a loud volume and not letting the microphone do the work can cause this as will singing long and loud. This is a common problem in larger congregations where the singing volume can be very loud and you try to sing loud enough to hear yourself.

What do I do if I loose my voice before or during the worship or preaching?

This is one of your nightmares! You are committed to the task, you get to the church and all is well right up to the point when you begin; and then, a croak, a squeak, a flat note, and two others completely missed! Inside you die and wish the floor would open up for you; but you must continue as everyone is listening even more intently now that they have heard your condition! (It is a good way to get the congregations attention)!
In some ways singers are more prone to this than preachers and it is harder to remedy the situation.

If you are song leading and have back up singers then they can save you! It is wise to have a lead back up singer that knows the song order and can step in for you when needed.

If you are a support singer then you can quietly step down or mouth the words and not sing. A soloist is in real trouble and has to do the best job possible using the microphone to help while trying to hold the song together and deliver the message.

Sing very lightly and do no extra fancy notes concentrate on getting words and individual notes out, and even talk it in time, instead of singing the notes can help cover your problem as the song goes through.

At the end, in an informal setting, an apology could be given with a request for prayer for the voice, but in larger groups and more set formal meetings there would be no room for this.

The use of the cold water glass can sometimes help but not always. Cold water tightens the muscles in the throat but warm water will relax and soothe helping to clear any mucus away. Whatever happens, you must not show your embarrassment and run off platform. It draws attention to yourself and away from the message you are trying to deliver.

Preachers are also in real trouble if this occurs, as they have no back up preachers to help them! They are committed to the task of delivering a message, so proceed with caution and try to use the microphone as much as possible for volume and effects. Work at getting each word out slowly and clearly. Try using a whiteboard and write out your points so that the message gets out.

Draw diagrams and use overheads, hand actions and mini-dramas could help out also. Choose a friendly creative person in the congregation to help act out a point to save you speaking about it! Keep your message to the main points, making it short and simple. If you feel a disaster coming on, then hand back to the song leader for some free praise and worship time or you could try some congregational prayer and sharing led by another leader.

"An excellent book for church leaders and also people of all ages with a desire to become more confident and skilled in their music ministry. Because music plays and important part in ushering in the presence of God; Mary has written vital keys to release people both spiritually and practically to their fullest potential. To firstly minister to the Lord, and also to be able to be a vessel used to bring Glory to Him. A very valuable book to have available in your church. It will inspire and motivate all who read it; well done Mary"
Pastor Les and Lynne Denton. Mangere Apostolic Church.

"This book is well written and yet with a simplicity that prevents confusion. This would be a must for any new Music Director"
Mr Russell Burk, Music Director. Katikati Chritsian Center.

"The presentation and layout is of a high standard, with print and illustrations very clear. There is a good flow between the subjects that are covered. It is well based on scripture and gives a very rounded approach to the area of vocal tuition. It is a springboard for leading from entertaining music to the other ministry uses of music. A book that needs to be read several times to absorb all its contents."
Lesley Lilley, Christian Life Center.

"This book has been a wonderful tool and aid to me with my professional singing lessons. The format and layout is simple and easy to understand. In addition, the way it is written is great because it's like having Mary right beside you talking and showing you exciting and rewarding music can be to a beginner or someone who is further down the track with music studies. All I can say is it's something everyone should have on their bookshelf if they are serious about music." Bruce Prince, Valley Road Church.

www.ingramcontent.com/pod-product-compliance
Lightning Source LLC
Chambersburg PA
CBHW072036060426
42449CB00010BA/2287